THE YOUNG PERSON'S ILLUSTRATED GUIDE TO AMERICAN FASCISM

THE YOUNG PERSON'S ILLUSTRATED GUIDE TO AMERICAN FASCISM

SUE COE
AND
STEPHEN F. EISENMAN

O/R

OR Books
New York · London

© 2025 Sue Coe and Stephen F. Eisenman

Published by OR Books, New York and London

Visit our website at www.orbooks.com

All rights information: rights@orbooks.com

All rights reserved. No part of this book may be reproduced or transmitted in any form or by any means, electronic or mechanical, including photocopy, recording, or any information storage retrieval system, without permission in writing from the publisher, except brief passages for review purposes.

First printing 2025

Cataloging-in-Publication data is available from the Library of Congress.

A catalog record for this book is available from the British Library.

Typeset by Lapiz Digital Services. Printed by BookMobile, USA, and CPI, UK.

Book design by Emma Ingrisani

paperback ISBN 978-1-68219-611-3 • ebook ISBN 978-1-68219-612-0

INTRODUCTION
HOW TO USE THIS BOOK

Before you read this book, it would be good to talk with family or friends about what democracy means to you. Fascism means the death of democracy, but you can't understand the first term without understanding the second. And because democracy is about WE, not ME, it's important to discuss it with others.

You probably know a lot about American democracy already, but to help your conversation, let's quickly review:

1. The United States is a "representative democracy," not a direct democracy. That means Americans elect people to make decisions for them. We let them decide big issues, like how much tax to pay, the best way to prevent the spread of diseases like Covid, and how to stop global warming.
2. Democracies endorse free speech and assembly. Without them, how could people decide what issues are most important and who to vote for?
3. In a democracy, laws apply equally to everybody. Nobody, not even the president, is above the law!
4. In a representative democracy, you need checks and balances. The president's power is limited by congress and the courts; the courts and congress by the president; and so on. Everybody checks everybody, so nobody gets too big. No kings allowed!

5. The U.S. is not just a representative democracy, it's a "federal" democracy. Though the people are sovereign, power is shared between the 50 states and the government in Washington, D.C. The idea is to prevent the central government from becoming too strong. Notice a theme?

Here's what you should talk about: How much democracy do you have in your daily life? Can you elect representatives to speak or act for you on the job or at school? Do you have freedom of speech everywhere you go? Do your parents (if you are young), teachers, friends and colleagues obey the same rules as you? Is there a system of checks and balances in workplaces, classrooms, or at home?

American democracy is quite limited

Were you surprised from your conversation to discover that our democratic freedoms are quite limited, especially when it comes to school, work, and home? Some people say the U.S. is only democratic every four years, when people vote for president. And even then, only partly, because our system of elections gives more say to states with small populations than big ones. That's on account of the Electoral College and the composition of the U.S. Senate. Wyoming, with a population of 580,000, gets three electoral votes for president. California, with 40 million, gets 54—that's 18 times as many. But California's population is 69 times as large as Wyoming's! (I'll let you do the rest of the math.)

According to the U.S. Constitution, every state is allotted two senators, regardless of size. That was discriminatory in 1780, but much more so today, with modern urbanization. The ten smallest, least urban U.S. states have a combined population of 7.5 million; the ten largest, 180 million. Yet their political power in the U.S. Senate is the same! And the U.S. House of Representatives is no more democratic. There, computer-generated algorithms drive gerrymandering, essentially allowing state legislators and party leaders to choose voters, rather than the other way around. The result is districts in which competitive elections are a near impossibility. And what's true at the federal level is also true at the state level. In Florida, roughly 36 percent of voters are registered Republicans, and 36 percent are Democrats (with the rest independent), but in the state legislature the division is 71 percent to 29 percent. (Republicans are better than Democrats at rigging elections.)

Free speech in the U.S. isn't very free either. If you own a TV or radio station or control a social media outlet—like Mark Zuckerberg or Elon Musk—you have tons of freedom of speech. If you are a corporation with billions to spend on advertising or political donations, your voice is REALLY LOUD! But if you are just an average person, nobody outside your immediate circle of family or friends will hear you or know what you think; your voice is a whisper. At work or school, you must be careful what you say to avoid getting into trouble. The freest speech you have is singing in the shower.

Decisions about war and peace in a representative democracy should be made deliberately and in consultation with voters. But in the U.S., popular sentiment is almost entirely ignored when it comes to foreign policy. Instead, supposed experts from foreign policy think tanks— their judgement clouded by working hand-in-glove with the arms and aerospace industries—make all the decisions, alongside politicians who receive the very same handouts. The result has been a succession of brutal, unpopular wars that have prevented progress on all other fronts. Israel's war against Palestine, for example, is widely unpopular according to polls, especially among younger Americans. Continued U.S. military support for the war is tantamount to endorsement of ethnic cleansing; Israeli officials have spoken openly about their desire to create a Gaza that is free of Palestinians.

Ongoing violence in the U.S. itself—nearly 50,000 dead every year from guns, 2,500 of whom are children—represents another case where democracy has been rejected by Republican and some Democratic congressmen, state legislators, and Supreme Court justices. Poll after poll indicates that the public wants meaningful gun control, but they almost never get it, thanks to political influence exercised by gun makers, the gun lobby and the political far right. Mass killings in the U.S. are literally a daily occurrence, creating a climate of fear in schools, churches, supermarkets, and especially synagogues and mosques.

If our democracy is so limited, why are Sue Coe and I so worried about protecting it from its opposite number, fascism? Isn't fascism—or its rudiments—already here? Good questions! Here's the answer: As imperfect as our government is, it could be a lot worse. Suppose, for example, there were officials who reviewed all your Facebook, Snapchat, Instagram, Reddit, TikTok, email, and text messages, and if they disapproved, they just erased them? Or worse: arrested you! What if you found out that being queer, Muslim, atheist, or a union member was suddenly illegal? Or how would you feel if you learned you could no longer read books by your favorite author because they couldn't be purchased anywhere, or even borrowed from the library? Suppose the nice boy in your high school biology class whom you have known since kindergarten, or the young barista who makes your latte just the way you like it, was suddenly gone—deported back to the country of their birth? What if the outcomes of elections were rigged, or if the loser claimed to be the winner and raised mobs to bully everybody into accepting the false claim? (That's what happened after the election of Joe Biden in 2020; Trump claimed he won and raised a mob to retain the presidency.) How would it be if you couldn't protest injustices because federal agents or even a private militia might arrest you or beat you up? Suppose you needed an abortion but couldn't get one because they were illegal? (Oops, that's already true in many U.S. states!)

Our existing democracy is badly flawed, but at least we can sometimes fix things that are broken. Think about the positive changes in the last sixty years. Here's three: the Voting Rights Act of 1964 ensured the franchise for Black people in the South. The Endangered Species Act of 1973 prevented the extinction of the bald eagle, the spotted owl, and many other animals. Protests by LGBTQ folks and their allies in the 1970s and '80s paved the way for laws and Supreme Court rulings (decades later) preventing discrimination and allowing gay marriage. Without the right to free speech and assembly, none of those changes would have happened. Without democracy, limited though it is, our future would look even dimmer than it appears today! Fascism kills democracy, and without democracy, peaceful change is impossible.

So what is fascism anyway, and what are some historical examples?

The word fascism derives from the Italian *fascio,* the name for the bundle of sticks carried by ancient Roman officials to beat into submission anybody who challenged their authority. A country gripped by fascism beats down its population until it acquiesces to dictatorial rule. Its ruler governs like a king, subject to few if any laws. (Not a king like the current King Charles of England; more like Atilla the Hun.) Citizens in fascist counties are encouraged to imagine a distant past when the country was great, while believing that the current, antidemocratic system will endure forever. In a fascist nation, the life of an individual is unimportant compared to the masses. The "masses" however, aren't the community or the collective—they're a population disciplined by fear and nationalist myth. Equally important for fascism is protecting "racial purity." It doesn't matter that there is no such thing as racial purity (all humans are biological equals); fascist rulers lie with abandon. Violence is freely used to prevent resistance and ensure compliance; political dissidents and racial, ethnic, or gender outliers may be sent to prisons or concentration camps or even killed.

Below is an abbreviated list of the distinguishing features of fascism. But remember that every fascist regime is a little different; if it comes to prevail in the U.S., it will have its own American characteristics. For one thing, people will waive the U.S. flag, not the Nazi swastika. In general, fascist governments:

1. Aim to bring all parts of their political and administrative systems to heel—no checks and balances
2. Use violence and plots to cripple opposition parties and control elections
3. Intimidate the press and take control of the media
4. Sponsor rallies and parades to celebrate the unity of a supposed racially pure nation

5. Uphold the "leadership principle." The nation's head is adored and called "The Leader"
6. Mock the rule of law and support the idea that might makes right
7. Rescind or limit women's rights: political, reproductive, and economic
8. Deny free sexual expression—sex is only for making babies and the pleasure of men
9. Denigrate science and promote lies and crazy conspiracy theories
10. Endorse the idea of white racial supremacy and make it the basis of policy

In 1921, the Italian dictator Benito Mussolini formed the National Fascist Party to unify and strengthen a nation badly diminished by World War I and economic recession. The Fascist Party celebrated discipline and violence and endorsed Imperialism—the bullying of weak states by strong ones to steal their wealth or control their markets and territory. Mussolini called himself *Il Duce* ("the leader") and insisted that everybody else also call him that. Fascist leaders are insecure, because the same arrogance and violence that brought them to power could topple them.

A version of fascism, called National Socialism or Nazism, arose at almost the same time in Germany. There, Adolf Hitler managed, by 1933, to gain power and begin a program of *Gleichshaltung*—"coordination" or Nazification. The goal was to bring all organs of state and civil society into conformity with Hitler's will. Control of the press, regimentation of everyday life, elimination of expressive freedoms, destruction of constitutional safeguards, control of trade unions, establishment of a dictatorial (one party) state and an end to the civil rights of minorities (especially

Jews) were all key aspects of Gleichshaltung. Hitler called himself *Der Führer* ("the leader") and insisted everybody salute him by raising their right arm above their shoulder and saying "*Sieg heil, mein Führer!*" or "Hail victory, my leader." As we all know, Hitler started World War II and was responsible for the Holocaust that murdered 6 million Jews.

Both Italian fascist and German Nazi leaders were ruthless. At first, they employed thugs, often former soldiers, to intimidate and even murder the leaders of unions and opposition organizations. Later, they maintained their own national corps of "shock troops" to undertake larger-scale bullying and violence. Their stated goals sounded lofty: to purify the social body, restore a stolen national glory, and establish an empire that would last millennia; but their theories were crackpot: that humanity was composed of biologically distinct races, with some innately superior to others; that violence and war were purifying; and that other nations, lacking racial purity, were certain to surrender to the superior fascist state.

But fascists could also be level-headed when they had to be. Their economic proposals generally brought support from the lower middle class, without alienating wealthy industrialists. Soon after gaining power, Mussolini and Hitler passed laws that boosted employment (though with low hourly wages) and subsidized big business. To succeed politically, they needed money and other assistance from industries, corporations, and the wealthy, as well as the masses; for the most part, they got it.

The fascist and Nazi quest for national and racial glory was thus also linked to the pursuit of profit. Fascism is completely compatible with capitalism (the generalized search for profit), so long as businesspeople don't get involved in politics, except when invited. The huge growth of weapons manufactures in Italy and Germany during the 1930s was good for the economy, and the fascists and Nazis gained public support because of it. Lots of people in both countries were willing to surrender democratic rights (including free speech and assembly) in exchange for economic stability. In remarkably short order, people accepted—sometimes even welcomed—the harassment, arrest, imprisonment and killing of Communists, Jews, queer people, Roma, the disabled, and others. Eventually, it all came crashing down; Hitler and Mussolini were like the biblical Samson who brought the temple down upon himself.

The end of World War II in 1945, marked the complete defeat of Italy, Germany, and the Japanese Empire, which was also fascist. (Japanese leaders claimed that Emperor Hirohito was divine, and that the *Yamato minzoku* people were racially superior.) The death toll was about 80 million in total. After that, it seemed for a while as if fascism was relegated to the dustbin of history and wouldn't ever reemerge. But in fact, it never entirely disappeared. Relatively few Nazi and Italian fascist leaders were arrested, imprisoned, or executed. Instead, government and corporate bosses became business executives or politicians in their own countries or else were quietly posted to university or government research centers in the U.S. or elsewhere. The technical expertise of Nazi scientists, especially in the areas of rocketry and atomic weapons research, was repurposed to aid the Cold War against the Soviet Union; their rabid anti-communism was used to train a generation of far-right agents to smother anti-colonial liberation struggles around the world.

Here's an example: Klaus Barbie, called the "butcher of Lyon" for his role in the deportation of at least 10,000 French Jews to Auschwitz, was given sanctuary first by the U.S. Army Counter-Intelligence Corps, and then by West German security services in exchange for covert anti-communist operations. Discovered by France—which sentenced him to death in absentia in 1947—Barbie was quickly sent by the U.S. to Bolivia, supported by "ratlines" of sympathetic Vatican officials and others. There, he assisted a succession of dictators, including Hugo Banzer and Luis García Meza, in developing brutal interrogation procedures, including torture, that would be used against democratic opposition figures during the U.S.-supported counterinsurgency program called Operation Condor (1975-83).

Fascism also survived in the person of the dictators Francisco Franco in Spain, António Salazar in Portugal, and others. Later, there were fascist governments—without the name—in Paraguay, Bolivia, Chile, Guatemala, South Africa, and elsewhere. More recently Brazil (under Bolsonaro), Hungary, Poland, India, and Israel (under Netanyahu and Likud) have embraced fascism without using the name. Putin's authoritarian regime in Russia also fits the definition of fascism. Italy's current prime minister belongs to a fascist party. The president of Argentina, Javier Milei, is fascist, though he calls himself "libertarian." Today, fascist ideas are on the rise in the United States, including among elected and aspiring leaders of the Republican Party: Donald Trump, J. D. Vance, Ron DeSantis, and too many Republican Senators and House members to list.

The roots of American fascism—slavery and segregation

The roots of current American fascism may be found in the the nation's origins. In 1787, thirteen former British colonies ratified a constitution that maintained "chattel" slavery—the ownership of Black people as tools for producing cotton, tobacco, sugar, and other commodities, as well as for domestic services. The slave regime was racist, totalitarian, and cruel. Families were often broken up by the sale of children, fathers, or mothers. Because they were legally considered property, enslaved women could be raped with impunity. And though "slave codes" usually prohibited murder, plantation masters were rarely prosecuted for the offense. Lacking legal protections for nearly half the population in slave holding states, American democracy was thus badly undermined from the beginning. The "three-fifths compromise" apportioned U.S. House seats and electoral votes based upon a state's free population, plus three-fifths of its slaves, even though the latter couldn't vote. The consequence was a significant electoral and judicial advantage for slave states that lasted until the Civil War. After the war, passage of the Fourteenth and Fifteenth Amendments to the U.S. Constitution in 1868 and 1870, guaranteeing birthright citizenship and voting rights for emancipated Black men (but not women), brought an interval of semi-democracy.

But Reconstruction, as it was called, proved short-lived. Already by 1877, southern Democrats, with the connivance of some northern Republicans, overturned Black civil rights and inaugurated a regime of segregation ("Jim Crow"), disenfranchisement, and violence. Democracy was once again undercut by racism. The Ku Klux Klan and similar hate groups were shock troops for wealthy, southern whites, and lynching was deployed as an instrument of terror. After a brief period of decline, the Klan roared back to life in the 1910s. By the '20s, the KKK had chapters all over the country, with as many as 5 million members. In 1925, 30,000 Klansmen in regalia marched down Pennsylvania Avenue in Washington.

Two years later, on Memorial Day, a rally of about 1,000 hooded and robed Klansmen was held in Jamaica, Queens, in New York City. Among the attendees was one Fred Trump, an aspiring New York City real estate baron, and later father of the ex-president. We know about it because the demonstration, ensuing riot, and Trump's arrest were reported the next day in *The New York Times.*

The first homegrown American fascists, the Ku Klux Klan, attacked Blacks, Jews, and Catholics. They posed for snapshots at lynchings, wrote about the "Lost Cause" (the supposed nobility of antebellum plantation life), cheered the racist movie *The Birth of a Nation* (D. W. Griffith, 1915), and published books with provocative and deceitful titles, like *The Passing of the Great Race* (Madison Grant, 1916) and *The Rising Tide of Color Against White World Supremacy* (Lothrop Stoddard, 1920). These books deeply influenced Nazi racial theorist Alfred Rosenberg and Hitler himself.

Until recently, American racial terror—slavery, segregation, and KKK violence—was not understood to be a version of fascism. It was instead seen as at best a tragic and at worst a criminal response to the harsh reality of the labor demands of cotton plantations in the American South. Slavery, according to this account, was America's "peculiar institution," fated to perish of its own contradictions: It was capital-intensive (enslaved people were expensive to buy and keep), inefficient (slaves lacked motivation and died young), and full of risk (enforced laborers escaped and rebelled when possible). Capitalist wage labor was its inevitable successor, and the unwinding of slavery's social and economic impacts was the achievement of multiple generations.

In fact, however, "racial fascism," as the poet and activist Amiri Baraka called it, was long a feature of European colonial conquest. Whether the victims were Native American, African, or South Asian, colonialism always conjured racial hierarchy and deployed violence to enforce domination of the subordinate group. Colonialism concentrated labor—whether slave or putatively free—in mines, factories, or latifundia, and mercilessly punished resistance. By this account, U.S. slavery, segregation, and Klan terror was not a short-lived mistake, but a continuation of the colonial order, and was allied with the pre-history of fascism in Europe.

Not everyone agrees on when a regime is fascist; it exists in the eye of the beholder. Not in the sense that it's a nighttime fantasy that can be evaporated by the light of dawn, but in the sense that its existence and impact differ depending upon who you are and where you stand. If you were an African American in the U.S. in the era of lynching and racial terror (roughly 1880–1950), or a Jew in Germany in the 1930s (or anywhere in Europe from 1938 to 1945), fascism was the dominant fact of social and political life. If you were a wealthy or powerful white person, or just a white person with a grudge, you'd likely have little interest in the characteristics of political or social systems; and you'd be largely unaffected by the oppression and violence suffered by others.

Ford, Hitler, and mass killing

In the 1920s, the car manufacturer Henry Ford published a newspaper, *The Dearborn Independent* (circulation 900,000), that propagated the notorious anti-Semitic libel, *The Protocols of the Elders of Zion*. His editorials stacked lie upon lie: "It is not merely that there are a few Jews among international financial controllers," he wrote, "it is that these world-controllers are *exclusively Jews* [original emphasis]." He added: "The motion picture influence of the United States, of the whole world, is exclusively under the control, moral and financial, of the Jewish manipulators of the public mind." Ford admired Hitler and the feeling was mutual. The *Führer* mentioned Ford approvingly in *Mein Kampf*, called him an "inspiration" in 1931, and seven years later awarded him the Grand Cross of the Order of Merit of the German Eagle. Ford's influence extended all the way to Auschwitz. His moving assembly line, first developed in 1913 at the Highland Park factory near Detroit, was the model for the rationalized killing machine used at Nazi death camps like Auschwitz and Treblinka. The cattle cars packed with Jews were the assembly lines; the gas chambers were the killing floors.

Decades later, the Nazi killing system was put to another use: feeding, killing and packaging animals as meat. American slaughterhouses, what's called "concentrated feeding operations," cram together tens or hundreds of thousands of animals in rows of barns. They're fed automatically, with occasional visits by workers. After a period of fattening or breeding, the animals are shipped off to another factory for slaughter by means of gas or captive bolts followed by throat cutting. Neither practice is cruelty-free—far from it. Fascism is a network of policies and practices that imparts death and suffering to animals as well as humans.

By the mid and late 1930s, links between American, German, and Italian fascism were clear. Dozens of U.S. organizations, including The Black Legion and the German American Bund espoused Nazi principles and trumpeted hatred for Blacks and Jews. In 1936, the Catholic priest

Charles Coughlin, who became a popular radio personality, proclaimed, "I take the road of fascism." In response, progressive scholars and writers including W. E. B. Du Bois, Langston Hughes, and Sinclair Lewis wrote about the dangers of fascism, and artists including William Gropper, Ben Shahn, Hugo Gellert, Philip Guston, Charles White, Elizabeth Catlett, and Ollie Harrington made works that challenged it.

American fascism didn't go unnoticed abroad. In Nazi Germany, the Klan was deeply appreciated, as J. H. Grill and R. Jenkins have shown in their essay "The Nazis and the American South in the 1930s: A Mirror Image?"[1] One German periodical of the 1930s described the Klan as "American fascism." Hitler applauded the South's "wholesome aversion for the Negroes and the colored races in general." Nazi newspapers and journals approved Southern laws mandating segregation, welcomed the lynching of Blacks, and supported Americans who opposed the "racial bastardization" of culture. Nazi leaders hated Black Olympic athletes, like Jesse Owens, and Black American music, which was sometimes heard in Berlin and other German cities. Among Hitler's favorite films was *Gone with the Wind* from 1939, which promoted the myth of the Lost Cause. "We will follow this example." Joseph Goebbels said, "and establish a great new social order based on the principle of slavery and inequality."

Notwithstanding the Nazi embrace of Southern segregation, few Southern politicians embraced Nazism, with the notable exception of Georgia Governor Eugene Talmadge, who in 1936 boasted of reading Hitler's *Mein Kampf* seven times. *The New Orleans Times-Picayune* in

---

1   *The Journal of Southern History*, vol. 58, pp. 667–94.

1938 stated, "Americans are against persecution of minority groups . . . Hitler will only gain respect in the U.S. if he stops persecuting the minority." Despite generally supporting segregation, almost no Southern newspapers of the period acknowledged similarities between Nazi and American racism. Black newspapers and journals, on the other hand, consistently made the parallel. In the magazine *Crisis*, founded by W. E. B. Du Bois, a 1938 editorial concluded: "The South approaches more nearly than any other section of the United States the Nazi idea of government by a 'master race' without interference from any democratic process."

In 1940, the isolationist and anti-Semitic "America First" Committee was formed by Charles Lindberg. Their slogan was already well known. For more than twenty years it was used by racists and people who hated foreigners, including the Klan. At an America First rally in Des Moines on September 11, 1941, Lindberg uttered a not-so-veiled threat to American Jews who supported U.S. entry into the war. It's worth quoting because of Lindberg's failed effort to avoid sounding like Hitler:

> "The three most important groups who have been pressing this country toward war are the British, the Jewish and the Roosevelt administration . . . Instead of agitating for war, the Jewish groups in this country should be opposing it in every possible way for they will be among the first to feel its consequences . . . Their greatest danger to this country lies in large ownership and influence in our motion pictures, our press, our radio, and our government."

A few months later, after the attack on Pearl Harbor, and the U.S. declaration of war against Germany and Japan, the America First movement collapsed. The public saw Lindberg and his followers as unpatriotic at best and traitors at worst. Formerly sympathetic politicians now gave America Firsters the cold shoulder. But the rejection was not permanent. Seventy-five years later, the slogan was popularized again by Donald Trump.

McCarthyism and the CIA

In the late 1940s and '50s, there was another major recrudescence of fascism in America. It began in Southern California, the epicenter of the emerging U.S. defense industry, and long a bastion of virulent anti-communism. There, a state senator named Jack Tenney led a series of investigations of communists (real and supposed), socialists, and even just liberals, in public schools, colleges and universities, labor unions and other civil society organizations. Books were banned from school libraries for insufficient patriotism and for the merest suggestion of sex education. Loyalty oaths for civil servants and professors were mandated. Tenney even travelled to Washington in 1947 to warn members of the U.S. House Un-American Activities Committee of the dangerously subversive activities of movie stars Charlie Chaplin, Fredrick March, Frank Sinatra, John Garfield, and Edward G. Robinson. The performers survived with their careers intact, though Chaplin—probably the greatest and most influential film artist who ever lived—was later barred from returning to the U.S. when his visa was revoked.

In 1947, HUAC began its own broad investigation of supposed communist infiltration of the movie industry. Eleven writers and directors were called to testify, and ten of them, later known as The Hollywood Ten, refused to answer questions. They were convicted of contempt of Congress, imprisoned for a year, and blacklisted from the industry. Energized by this anti-communist zealotry, the newly elected Republican senator from Wisconsin, Joe McCarthy, in 1950 leveled charges that the U.S. State Department employed 205 communists or communist sympathizers (the number later changed to 57, then 81, and then 108) in high-level posts, creating a national security risk. The charges were phony, but they cast McCarthy into the national limelight. He used it to launch still more investigations—today generally characterized as witch hunts—that had the effect of destroying careers and instilling fear in anyone who ever held progressive political views.

When Republican Dwight Eisenhower was elected president in 1952 and the Democrats lost control of Congress, McCarthy was empowered to run his own investigations. He and his chief counsel, Roy Cohn, hounded targets in and out of government, even driving one victim to suicide. Finally, in 1954, McCarthy himself was investigated by his fellow Senators over a relatively minor charge of improperly recommending a U.S. Army private for promotion. The resulting Army–McCarthy hearings, televised nationally, proved the senator's undoing. After yet another attempt by McCarthy at character assassination, a lawyer for the army, Joseph Nye Welch, called McCarthy's bluff. He famously said: "Senator. You've done enough. Have you no sense of decency, Sir, at long last? Have you left no sense of decency?" The spell appeared to be broken, and the witch hunt ended.

In fact, it had not. Though the pace slackened, there continued to be investigations of real and supposed communists in government, entertainment, and education. The Black athlete, actor and singer Paul Robeson was called before HUAC in 1956 and questioned about his support for civil rights, Soviet Russia, and U.S. communists. He gave as good as he got: "I am here because I am opposing the neo-Fascist cause which I see arising in these committees. You are like the Alien and Sedition Act [passed in 1798, which restricted free speech]. Jefferson could be sitting here, and Frederick Douglass could be sitting here, and Eugene Debs could be here . . . . you are the un-Americans, and you ought to be ashamed of yourselves." Robeson was barred from travel and performance abroad, and blacklisted in the U.S. His passport was restored to him after a Supreme Court ruling in 1958, and he undertook a concert tour abroad. But by then, his mental and physical health was broken, and he never fully recovered.

The witch hunt now extended to queer people as well. In April 1953, during the height of the "Lavender Scare," President Eisenhower issued Executive Order 10450 banning employment by the U.S. Government of anyone engaged in "criminal, infamous, dishonest, immoral, or notoriously disgraceful conduct, habitual use of intoxicants to excess, drug addiction, [and] sexual perversion." The last prohibition was aimed at queer communities. The result was the dismissal of thousands of homosexual and trans federal employees, and hundreds of thousands more queer people across the country after state and local governments passed copycat laws. It would take a "sexual revolution" in the 1960s to begin to change American attitudes toward gender-nonconforming persons, and another generation still before they were granted greater—though still not full—civil rights.

Fascist avatar: Trump

In 2016, fascism returned to the U.S. in the person of Donald Trump, but he was just its avatar. "America First" was Trump's campaign slogan along with "Make America Great Again." A few months after his inauguration, the two slogans were heard at a white supremacist "Unite the Right" rally in Charlottesville, Virginia. A couple of hundred Klan members, "neo-Nazis," neo-Confederates, and several far-right militia groups marched through the University of Virginia campus chanting, "You will not replace us," "Jews will not replace us," and "Blood and Soil." They assaulted students and counterprotesters. The following day, still more marched and chanted racist, anti-Semitic, and homophobic slogans and clashed with hundreds of counterprotesters. At the height of the fracas, a twenty-year-old neo-Nazi drove his car into a group of anti-fascists, killing Heather D. Heyer, a thirty-two-year-old paralegal from Charlottesville. That morning, David Duke, a former KKK Grand Wizard, called the protests "a turning point for the people of this country . . . . We're going to fulfill the promises of Donald Trump. That's why we voted for Donald Trump, because he said he's going to take our country back." Trump himself made various contradictory comments about the event, eventually settling on "Not all of those people were white supremacists by any stretch," adding there were "very fine people on both sides."

Trump did not become a fascist when he rode down the Trump Tower escalator to announce his presidential candidacy in 2015. He was arguably born and raised one. His father, Fred, was a racist who taught Donald the ropes of the real estate business and bankrolled him. In 1973, Fred and Donald were found to have violated the U.S. Fair Housing Act by refusing to rent to Black and other nonwhite applicants for rentals at 39 Trump-owned properties in New York City. Donald was represented at the resulting civil trial by none other than Roy Cohn, Joe McCarthy's bulldog. The case ended with a consent decree requiring the Trumps to stop discriminating and to actively seek out nonwhite renters. Cohn remained Donald's lawyer, mentor, and confidant for the next dozen years, ending only with Cohn's death in 1986.

Trump's notoriety later increased when, in 1989, he placed a full-page ad in *The New York Times* demanding the death penalty for the young men accused and later convicted of the rape of Trisha Meili, the so-called "Central Park jogger." The men were exonerated, and their convictions overturned in 2002; they received a financial settlement from the city in 2014. When asked, in 2019, if he felt sorry for his actions considering subsequent events, Trump stuck to his story: "You have people on both sides of that," he said at the White House. "They admitted their guilt."

The 2020 election and its aftermath

By election year 2020, fascist organizing in the U.S. had advanced further than at any time since the height of the Klan a century before. The Southern Poverty Law Center documented hundreds of far-right anti-government and other hate groups across the United States, though the number of actual members is difficult to know since some groups are more public than others. Many exist online only—or at least until someone in the online community decides to carry out a mooted campaign of violence or intimidation. On April 30, 2020, dozens of heavily armed Michigan militia members occupied the capitol in Lansing to bully legislators to vote against pandemic-protection measures. Trump regalia was everywhere, and the president later praised the mob as "very good people, but very angry." Similar demonstrations occurred in other states, though on a smaller scale. When asked in a presidential debate if he endorsed white supremacist militias including the Proud Boys—storm troopers in waiting—Trump looked at the audience but spoke to the militias, saying "stand back and stand by." It was a stunning reply, never modified or retracted.

On the eve of the election in November, pundits expected a Democratic landslide. Trump's poll numbers were way down—largely the result of his poor response to the Covid pandemic. There was also speculation that Trump had turned off suburban and women voters—including Republicans—with his constant lies, racism, sexism, homophobia and hatred of foreigners. The results of the vote, however, did not entirely confirm that view. Trump was soundly defeated, but not by as large a margin as expected, and the Democrats lost seats in the House. Trump claimed the presidential vote was rigged. Nevertheless, the morning after election night, it was widely felt that Trump would soon accept defeat and fade from view.

Not quite. January 6, 2020, released all the fascist toxins that Trump so carefully nurtured and inspired: MAGA ultranationalism, America First-ism, racism, anti-Semitism, lying, a leadership cult, and extrajudicial violence. Still denying his electoral defeat, Trump urged a crowd of more than 10,000 at the Ellipse, south of the White House, to "fight like Hell" to "take back our country" from "bad people." The assembled mob, he said, was "special" and they must march to the Congress to lend Republicans "the kind of pride and boldness they need to take back our country," and he would be marching with them. Before he finished his speech, a contingent led by the Proud Boys—whom Trump had earlier asked to "stand by"—reached the capital perimeter and began a siege.

What followed—with Trump contentedly watching on TV from the White House—was several hours of mayhem outside and inside the Capitol complex. The mob terrorized legislators, threatened to hang the Republican vice president, and caused a temporary suspension of the electoral vote count. One intruder was shot dead, many capital police were injured, and several other officers later died of various causes: shock, stroke, and suicidal despair caused by the riot. Finally, in the early hours of January 7, 2021, the electoral vote count on the House floor was resumed. Though a total of 147 Republicans cast ballots to reject the votes of several key swing states, they were outnumbered by Democrats and a minority of Republicans, and Biden became President-elect. The fever of rising fascism seemed to have broken, and representative democracy secured.

The ledger book of Trumpian fascism

"Unite the Right" in Charlottesville in August 2017 and the Capitol insurrection of January 6, 2021 were like bookends, with significant fascist initiatives in between. In his four years in office, Trump and his Republican supporters in Congress packed the courts—including the Supreme Court—with incompetent or corrupt flunkies, succeeding at last in ending the right to abortion and granting presidents (Trump v. United States) near dictatorial powers. They attacked the independence of federal departments by calling them agents of the "deep state," and sought to enact a policy of *Gleichschaltung*, bringing all sectors of government—no matter how large or small—into lockstep with Trump's policy and persona. They were only partly successful in the effort. For example, they failed to remove job protections for civil service employees because they began the effort too late in the term. That initiative, outlined by the Federalist Society's Project 2025 governance manual, awaits a second Trump term.

As president, Trump repeatedly lashed out against the press, calling reporters who asked him hard questions "enemies of the people." With the enthusiastic cooperation of Rupert Murdoch, Trump established Fox News as an informal state propaganda office (Tucker Carlson was his Joseph Goebbels). No lie was too small or too big, including that the Covid virus was something "we have tremendous control of" (March 15, 2020), that it was "like the regular flu," (April 1, 2020), and was "going to disappear" (October 10, 2020). It has been estimated that roughly 40 percent of the 400,000 Covid deaths during Trump's presidency could have been avoided, had protective measures been taken sooner. After the police killing of George Floyd in Minneapolis in May 2020, Trump regularly called civil rights protesters "thugs," "terrorists" and "anarchists" even though more than 93 percent of the nearly 8,000 demonstrations across the country were entirely peaceful, according to researchers at the Armed Conflict Location & Event Data Project at Princeton University. Trump tried to deploy 10,000 active-duty troops to quell the protests—it's usually illegal to use the American military within the U.S.—but Secretary of Defense Esper and Chairman of the Joint Chiefs of Staff Miley managed to thwart the plan.

Fascist violence, American style

By the time of Biden's inauguration on January 20, 2021, the fascist tide at last seemed to have receded. But once more, the announcement of democracy's salvation was premature at best. Trump's propaganda machinery remained intact, and Republican voters still today believe his lies about the 2020 election; accept his claims that the 91 felony charges against him (and 34 convictions, so far) are the result of lies and persecution; and endorse the view that President Biden deserves to be arrested and jailed. In the meanwhile, fascist violence—of the peculiarly American kind—has continued to rage.

Nearly every politically driven mass murder in the past six years was committed by a lone wolf, far-right extremist. They include the killing of 11 members of a Pittsburgh synagogue in October 2018; the El Paso murder of 22 Latinos in August 2019; the Buffalo killings of 10 Black people in a supermarket in May 2022; the Colorado Springs murder of five at the Pulse LGBTQ nightclub in November of that year; and the killing of seven and wounding of dozens more in Highland Park, Illinois on July 4, 2022. That latter murder spree, perpetrated by twenty-one-year-old Robert (Bobby) Crimo, is exemplary of those before and since.

Despite an Illinois law preventing mentally ill individuals from obtaining a gun license, Crimo, with the help of his gun-loving father, bought at least five guns, including a pair of semiautomatic rifles. (A year earlier, he attempted suicide and threatened to kill his family.) In late September 2020, Bobby attended a Trump rally in Northbook, Illinois. On January 2, 2021, four days before the capital insurrection, Crimo joined other Trump supporters to greet the soon-to-be ex-president at an airport. On June 27, 2021, he posted a video of himself dancing and draped with a Trump flag. Sometime later, he had the number "47" tattooed on his face and painted on the side of his car. If Trump is reelected in 2024, he will be the 47th president, though if the numbers are transposed, they mark the date of the Highland Park shootings, the Fourth of July, a day set aside for celebrating American democracy.

In YouTube and other postings just prior to his rampage, Crimo revealed his identification with soldiers, spies, assassins (Lee Harvey Oswald) and warriors—and especially with the German SS. After the massacre in Highland Park, he drove up to another famously Democratic stronghold, Madison, Wisconsin, with the intention of shooting up their July 4 parade too. Fortunately, he abandoned that plan when he got there and returned to the scene of the crime, where he was captured.

Was the ongoing Trump saga—the former president's unrelenting "stop the steal" lies, claims of persecution, exhortations to "take our country back," and invitations to violence—the cause of the shootings? We may never know for certain, but the combination of mental illness, far-right politics, gun fanaticism, and Trump adoration has become common among mass shooters. Fascist violence isn't always state-sponsored; it can be conducted by isolated individuals—almost always men—angry at their own economic precarity, sexual insecurity, and political debility, and inspired by supposed supermen. The assassination attempt by Thomas Crooks on Trump himself in July 2024, fits that mold. The would-be killer was conservative, a loner, a gun-lover, and psychologically scarred.

In his book *Male Fantasies* (1987), Klaus Theweleit described the transformation of decommissioned German soldiers after World War I into mercenary militias called *Freikorps*. Those bands were responsible for political assassinations and the brutal repression of protesting German workers, communists, feminists, and social democrats. By the late '20s, they became the fascist storm troopers (*Sturmabteilung*) that enabled Hitler's rise to power. Some became prominent Nazis, like Rudolf Höss, commandant of the Auschwitz concentration and death camps.

Many of the men studied by Theweleit were subjected to stern discipline as children—part of a typically pathological, fin-de-siècle Prussian upbringing—and then further brutalized as soldiers in wartime trenches. Consequently, they developed a sense that they had been hollowed out, or that they had been overcome by an "alien within." This alien-being was hungry and dangerous, and could find relief only in violence, especially against a crowd. While the solider was stern, bounded, firm and resolute, the crowd was vivid, thriving, shapeless, feminine, social, communal, and sensual—everything he was not—and had to be destroyed.

While there is no easy way to map a wide-ranging study like Theweleit's of the literature and psychopathology of World War I veterans, onto the mind and behavior of a young, mass shooter today, the preoccupations of the Highland Park killer are telling. He was fascinated by assassinations, school shootings, the SS, spies, guns, knives, and militias. Like the young fascists in *Male Fantasies* who emerged in interwar Europe and became fascist *freikorps* mercenaries, SA and SS, troops, Crimo was mentally scarred, hated crowds, despised Jews, immigrants, and women, and was primed to follow the directions of a charismatic leader. Is there something about American society, like the German culture described by Theweleit, that produces young men like Crimo and Crooks?

The political economy of current fascism

For the last several decades, the American right has been improbably forged from two forces: free-market (or "neoliberal") capitalism, and Christian nationalism and other forms of far-right extremism. Advocates of the first aim to ensure the highest possible profits for the longest possible time, regardless of the human or environmental consequences. Because of the climate crisis, this posture poses existential risks. Unlimited economic growth and unending profits are simply incompatible with environmental responsibility and human survival. For that reason, the fossil fuel industry, along with its confederates in the weapons, aerospace, steel, and home building industries, has been waging a legal war against any environmental regulations that would curb growth. Maintaining a conservative Supreme Court, like the present one, that consistently sides with industry against labor and the environment, has been for them a political priority. With three Supreme Court appointments in just four years, Trump delivered big time in his first term. More appointments would mean fewer regulations, more profits and even more CO_2 and environmental degradation.

The goal of the second group, the far-right Christian nationalists, anti-abortionists, militias, and conspiracy theorists, is to establish a new nation of white, Christian, Aryan, or "legacy" Americans who will reclaim the economic and political power they believe was taken from them by a cabal of Jews, Blacks, feminists, queers, globalists, and other elites. Their cultism (QAnon, Stop the Steal, Replacement Theory, anti-vax), gun-rights militancy, and religious enthusiasm has little in common with the secularism and public reserve of the company heads, lawyers, bankers, lobbyists, and advertising executives who comprise the corporate faction of U.S. conservatism, but they share one fundamental principle: that the only salient economic and political unit is the individual, the family, or the corporation considered as an individual.

For current, neoliberal capital, this means that state or federal programs to regulate production, improve social welfare, and protect the environment are both non-sensical and counterproductive; they are based on the mistaken premise that societies exist and have collective interests that need to be safeguarded. For the Christian-nationalist far right, (gun-loving, anti-abortion, and the rest), an exclusive focus on individuals, families and religious brethren means that any social groupings that oppose their apocalyptic vision must be cast aside if not eliminated. Social movements of feminists, queers, Blacks, Jews, socialists, secularists, and environmentalists are anathema—they must be destroyed. (In fact, of course, it is the very deregulation and public disinvestment championed by large corporations and their political allies that has immiserated so many Americans and driven them to the Trumpian far right.) This mixture of monopoly capitalist and far-right-populist extremism is dangerous. When their combined worldview is trumpeted by the former president, his vice-presidential running mate, and their congressional and mass-media followers and apologists, the affiliation with fascism becomes apparent.

Republican leaders in Congress, and in state governor's mansions, have embraced fascism with enthusiasm, without of course, naming it. The clearest example is Florida, where Governor Ron DeSantis presides over a one-party supermajority in the state house, the result of effective gerrymandering. There, he has illegally fired elected officials who disagree with him; eliminated two Black-majority Congressional districts (in clear violation of the state constitution); organized a special police force—answerable only to him—that arrested about two dozen former felons (poor and Black) who inadvertently violated Florida voting law;

kidnapped and transported asylum-seekers to northern states; effected a permanent ban on future mask or vaccine mandates; passed draconian laws and administrative edicts controlling what university professors and students can and cannot say in the classroom and on campus; ended the right to abortion after six weeks of pregnancy; ostracized and banned trans students (especially trans athletes); silenced discussion of LGBTQ issues in schools; facilitated book bans in school and public libraries; criminalized much public protest; and alienated the state's biggest private employer (Disney) over its support for gay employees. Fascism can grow as quickly as cancer and as widely as a pandemic. It is fatal to democracy.

Trump and Hitler

Recently, it's become common to ask whether if elected, Trump will become a new Hitler. (The idea was first broached by J. D. Vance in 2016.) Clearly, there are similarities in their rhetoric. On Veteran's Day, 2023, Trump addressed an audience of Republican voters in New Hampshire and made the following promise:

> "In honor of our great Veterans on Veteran's Day, we pledge to you that we will root out the Communists, Marxists, Fascists, and Radical Left Thugs that live like vermin within the confines of our Country, lie, steal, and cheat on Elections, and will do anything possible, whether legally or illegally, to destroy America, and the American Dream."

A few weeks later, Trump extended his vilification: "Illegal immigration is poisoning the blood of our nation. They're coming from prisons, from mental institutions, from all over the world. Without borders and fair elections, you don't have a country. Make America great again."

The idea that human "vermin" and outsiders were "poisoning the blood" of good Germans was frequently expressed by Hitler, Goebbels, Himmler, and other Nazis. For example, in *Mein Kampf*, Hitler demanded expulsion from Germany of foreign elements, especially Jews and socialists: "While the flower of the nation's manhood was dying at the front [in World War I], there was time enough at home at least to exterminate this vermin [*"das Ungeziefer"*]. But, instead of doing so, His Majesty the Kaiser held out his hand to these hoary criminals . . . so the viper could begin his work again." After visiting a Jewish ghetto in Lodz, Poland in 1939, Goebbels wrote: "We have to make surgical cuts here, very radical ones. Otherwise, Europe will perish from the Jewish disease." A year or so later, just as the murder of Jews in Eastern Europe was ramping up, SS leader Heinrich Himmler said: "I am obeying the highest law by doing my duty. Man must defend himself against bedbugs and rats, against vermin." At the end of the war, Hitler looked back over the previous decades and summed up his aims: "To exterminate the vermin throughout Europe."

When questioned about the Nazi resonance of the word "vermin," Trump's spokesman Steven Cheung affirmed it while denying it: "[T]hose who try to make that ridiculous assertion are clearly snowflakes grasping for anything because they are suffering from Trump Derangement Syndrome and their entire existence will be crushed when President Trump returns to the White House." Realizing that the phrase "entire existence will be crushed" sounded Nazi, Cheung amended his statement. He was only referencing his opponents' "sad, miserable existence," he said, not their "entire existence." Asked about the Hitlerian resonance of "poisoning the blood," Trump said that Hitler meant something completely different, and that he had never read anything by Hitler. (In 1990, Ivana Trump told a *Vanity Fair* interviewer that her husband kept a volume of Hitler's speeches in a cabinet by his bed.)

The former president has said that when he's elected, he will use the Justice Department to indict political opponents and exact "retribution." He would invoke the Insurrection Act "on Day One" to round up thousands of undocumented immigrants and bar public protest about it. To help him, he'd hire a group of lawyers whose allegiance was to him alone. (No more checks and balances.) He would, as promised during his first term, end civil service protection for thousands of federal workers, so they could be fired if they were disloyal to Trump. He'd make sure all education was patriotic; restrict abortion by allowing states to enact even the most extreme bans; police gender identity; and challenge the rules of postelection succession. Trump pledged to invade or bomb Mexico to stop drug trafficking. (That has now become a common Republican talking point.) He rejects the facts of climate change, and promises to "drill, drill, drill." He would thus stand with his party in implicitly endorsing heat waves, massive forest fires, wars over drinking water, rising seas, flooding, mass migration, species extinction, the collapse of major agricultural systems and global starvation. Republican Party politics has become a death cult.

Most of all, Trump, like Hitler, deploys "the big lie" to gain prestige and power. In a representational democracy, the direct use of violence to dominate the mass of the population is impossible; legal safeguards are robust enough to prevent it. That's why propaganda (the lie), is so essential to aspiring dictators like Trump, and the bigger the lie, the better. In

Mein Kampf, Hitler wrote: "In the big lie there is always a certain force of credibility; because the broad masses of a nation . . . in the primitive simplicity of their minds, more readily fall victims to the big lie than the small lie, since they themselves often tell small lies in little matters but would be ashamed to resort to large-scale falsehoods." There's a superficial plausibility in the argument. But the success of political lying is not due to the "primitive simplicity" of citizens; it's a result of the conscious embrace of liars by a politically disaffected minority.

The liar is judged by them to be a loveable rogue, willing to say what average people won't, to attract followers and power. Then, upon gaining authority, the fascist leader enacts policies that seem to validate the lies, attracting still more support. The pattern was common with Hitler, as Hannah Arendt demonstrated in her book *The Origins of Totalitarianism* (1948). It's also true for Trump. After deceitfully claiming a few thousand poor immigrants from Mexico constituted an enemy invasion, Trump in October 2018, sent 5,200 U.S. troops to stop them, making his lie sound true. After all, why would anybody call the troops without military justification? Trump also claimed to be the victim of a wide-ranging conspiracy to steal the 2020 election. Now that he has been indicted for it (among other crimes), he claims vindication—the plots against him have been proven real! To his most ardent followers he's a prophet who inspires devotion, even love.

Lesser lights than Trump have deployed lies in a similar fashion. When Florida Governor Ron DeSantis wanted to pass new laws to further suppress Black voting, he claimed widespread election fraud. To bolster his preposterous claim (he himself stated the opposite immediately after the 2020 election) DeSantis created a new police force to prevent election fraud. The consequent arrests validated the premise of the lie, and the would-be fascist was vindicated. The fact that judges have dismissed most of the charges, indicates that DeSantis's takeover of the state judicial system was incompletely realized.

Even if Trump's and DeSantis's lies about immigration, prosecution, and voting were not universally accepted as truths, they were nevertheless effective in shifting public policy. Joe Biden's immigration strategy today is little different from Trump's. The former president's remaining court cases look as if they will be postponed until after the election, when he will be in a position—if he wins—to quash them. Voter suppression in Florida, as in other Republican states, continues to gain ground, despite the obvious fatuity of claims about election fraud. Though legal safeguards remain, the rule of law has been badly weakened by the four years of Republican rule from 2016 to 2020. If Trump is returned to power, his Hitlerian lies—that the election in 2020 was rigged and that he has been victim of a Biden/Harris witch hunt—will seem to have been validated. At that moment, Trump, himself and his millions of followers will believe he is a prophet. And the greater his confidence and popular support, the more likely he will resort to the political violence he frequently intimates. "I will be your retribution," Trump likes to repeat. When that becomes true, fascism will have taken full force and democracy killed.

Conclusion

Don't close this book—not until you have talked to your family or friends about what it would mean if the U.S. rejected representative democracy and chose fascism. It shouldn't be hard to envision, because we have already experienced four years of Trump and the far-right programs of current Republican governors and state legislators. We have also been plunged into war (by proxy), courtesy of the current Democratic administration. Here are five current examples of fascist policies:

1. Florida, Georgia, Mississippi, Virginia, Tennessee, Texas, and other states passed laws that ban teaching that racism was fundamental to the nation's founding. Other states, including Alabama and South Dakota have new laws preventing teaching about gender or sexuality. A law in Texas requires the teaching of "informed American patriotism" and acknowledgement of "the deepest and noblest purposes of the United States and Texas." Most U.S. states, including Democratic-led New York and California, have passed laws that require government retaliation against the movement to boycott, divest and sanction Israel for its actions against Palestine. These laws undermine free speech and the right to protest.
2. In nearly every Republican state in the U.S., legislators have rejected established medical recommendations and passed bills to deny transgender and nonbinary teens access to age-appropriate care. There are also new laws banning trans or cross-dressed public performances, though some of these have been stopped or suspended by courts because they violate first amendment, free speech protections. A few states have sought to limit civil rights protections to queer people, enabling discrimination by businesses, private employers and even doctors and hospitals.
3. In every state where Republicans control state government, abortion has been banned or severely restricted. The only exceptions are states which passed statewide referenda in support

of abortion rights. That happened in Ohio and Kansas. More ballot initiatives are expected in six more Republican states in 2024, including Florida and Missouri. Republican officials in those and other states have responded to popular demands for abortion rights by challenging the language of the measures and trying to rescind laws permitting citizen sponsored ballot initiatives!

4. The American Library Association reported that in 2023, there were nearly 700 attempts to censor materials in public libraries, affecting more than 1,900 individual titles. Most of the attacks were upon books that in some way concern race, gender, or sex. In the 2022–23 school year, PEN America identified 3,362 cases of books being removed from school libraries. Nobel Prize winner Toni Morrison and Booker Prize winner Margaret Atwood were among the most frequent targets of censorship.

5. Many U.S. states have active private militias. They are found especially in rural areas and have taken advantage of lax gun-control laws. Texas and Florida, both Republican states, have the most registered guns of any states and the least restrictive gun laws. The 12 states with the highest rates of gun mortality, according to the CDC, are all Republican, except for New Mexico. The cities with the most gun-homicide deaths, based on research by the Center for American Progress, are all in Southern and midwestern states with lax gun laws. All are Republican. The map of increased gun deaths roughly matches the map of highest cancer deaths: the latter are due to poverty, poor access to medical care, and high levels of toxic contamination from the oil and gas industry; the former from eased rules about buying, carrying, and concealing weapons. Fascism in the U.S. is manifested today by mass shootings and spikes in preventable deaths.

Did your conversation about America under the shadow of fascism surprise you, scare you, make you angry, or encourage you to take action to prevent it? All of the above? That's great!

It's still possible to stop fascism in its tracks and improve American democracy at the same time. Here's five ways to do it:

1. Vote for Harris and Walz in November. They will be building upon Biden's mixed legacy. He began his term as the most progressive president since Roosevelt: His combined American Jobs Plan and American Families Plan totaled more than $4 trillion and would have been bigger and more consequential than the New Deal. The proposals included money for childcare and pre-kindergarten education, paid family leave, free tuition to community colleges, expanded medical coverage under Obamacare, a massive increase in spending to limit climate change and higher taxes on the rich and corporations. After a period of negotiating with himself and a pair of weak Democratic senators, the much reduced "Infrastructure Bill" and "Inflation Reduction Act" were signed into law. Biden unfortunately undermined some of his climate change achievements by allowing oil and gas exploration to proceed at a record clip.

    Two years into Biden's term, things went from ok-but-not-great to worse. Though the U.S. economy continued to strengthen, foreign affair went sideways. Despite advance warning, the U.S. president did not intervene to stop the war in Ukraine, and after Putin's drive to Kiev was thwarted, failed to seize the opportunity to negotiate peace. In fact, Biden blocked all paths to an early, negotiated settlement and still today (as of October 2024) remains opposed to talks with Putin. And then, in October 2023, following the despicable Hamas attack on civilians in Israel, Biden flew to Israel to embrace Israeli President Netanyahu and give him carte blanche for full-scale invasion. Now Biden is complicit in a genocide, and if he lives long enough, he may find himself in the dock of the International Criminal Court in The Hague.

Harris has not distinguished herself from Biden, but nevertheless merits election. The alternative candidate is anti-union, anti-worker, anti-woman, anti-queer, anti-Black, and anti- all nonwhites. Trump's climate policies will exacerbate the ongoing catastrophe. Plus, he would foreclose even the possibility of political and social change by undermining rights to free speech and assembly. That's what he has promised. Fascism kills democracy, however vitiated.

2. Join a community-based organization that's trying to improve democracy. It could be a group that supports environmental protection, human rights, animal rights, abortion rights or children's rights. It could be an organization that helps incarcerated or formerly incarcerated people. There are CBOs that aim to reduce cancer deaths, clean beaches, minimize the use of disposable plastic, and feed poor people. All are examples of grassroots democracy. The more you participate in democracy, the more it grows and spreads.

3. Protest the wars. The U.S. is fighting a proxy war against Russia without ever consulting Congress or the American people. The stalemated results have been devastating for the whole world, and yet the U.S. and Ukraine reject negotiations. The Israeli war against Palestine has been a catastrophe. While Harris's policy if elected is unclear, Trump has promised only to "let Israel finish the job" in Gaza. Acceptance of mass death is a sign of fascism.

4. Talk to your neighbors, even if you have different political beliefs—even if they support the orange-colored fascist. Few people are completely lost or ineducable!
5. Take care of your physical and mental health. Walk, run, swim, play sports. Read, write, listen to music, watch movies, look at art (or make art) and go to the theatre. Meditate. Eat healthy—vegan is best for you, the planet, and the animals. Most of all, remain vigilant! Only you can prevent fascism!

THE POLITICAL ART OF SUE COE

ART FOR ART'S SAKE VS. POLITICAL ART

For nearly 200 years, there have been debates between those who support "art for art's sake," and those who endorse art that represents social, historical, religious, or political subjects. The former position was never as straightforward as it sounds. During periods when art was expected to be moralistic or didactic, or serve the interests of church or state, the refusal of an artist to create such works was intensely political. Depending upon the context, art for art's sake could imply rule-breaking, political, or religious dissidence, and even revolution. By the same token, art that engaged approved subjects was sometimes so formulaic and predictable, that its content disappeared. It became meaningless—an unintentional or failed example of art for art's sake!

Nevertheless, there's a long-time bias against art with clear, political meaning. "If you want to send a message," says the art critic, "write a letter!" But today, that view is less often held. The reason is that the subtleties of art for art's sake—especially abstract or nonrepresentational art—are often invisible against a backdrop of mediated mayhem. Try as we might to escape the wars, climate disasters, and rising tide of fascism at home and abroad, these debacles enter our consciousness at all hours—through our smartphones and otherwise—including when we are engaged in aesthetic contemplation. When that happens, all subtleties of form disappear. Only an interventionist, or politically engaged, art can compete with our internal doom scrolling and fully engage our minds and senses.

"In Crowd"

"Making A Fascist"

"Capitalism"

"Jump Jim Crow"

Henry Ford, Hitlers hood ornament

"Ford Hitler"

"Witch Hunters"

"Dark Money"

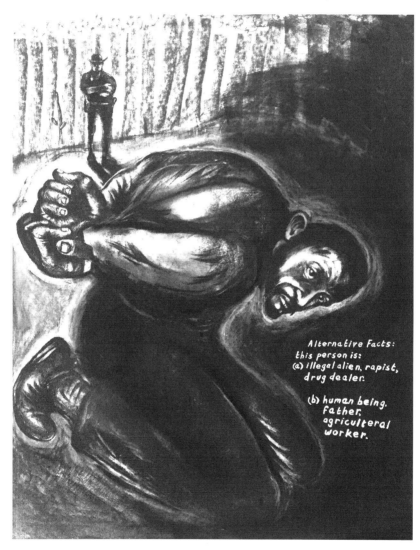

"The Wall"

"American Concentration Camp Creche"

"The Reward for Just Following Orders"

"The Chorus Line"

"Hungry"

"Flowing Backwards"

"Resisting"

"Triumph of Death Cult"

"Scrotus"

"She Was Just Following Orders"

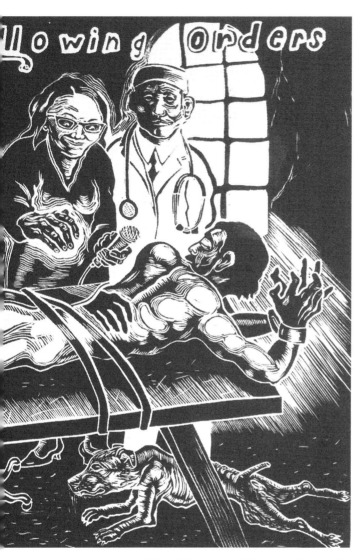

"They Were Just Following Orders"

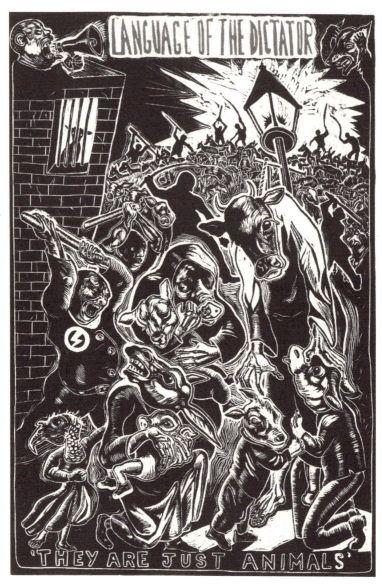

"Language of the Dictator"

"Political Canines"

THE ARTIST AS POLITICAL THINKER

Sue Coe has been making political art for more than 50 years, since she received an MA at the Royal College of Art in London and moved to New York City. Her knowledge of her subjects—U.S. politics, war, domestic violence, human and animal oppression, public health, environmental degradation, civil rights—is broad and deep, but it's the understanding of a well-read artist, not a politician or professor.

Consider two linocuts, chockablock with images and ideas: *JBS—Climate Butcher* (see p. 177) and *Stock Market* (p. 133). In the first print, some animals drown while others row toward safety in a flooded world; billboards of hamburgers and fried chicken remind us that animal agriculture is one of the major culprits in global CO_2 increases and rising sea levels; the moon and sun fight like debating politicians while cities are inundated. In the second, print, we see a trading floor crammed with men. Their mouths are agape, and their hands clutch at anything with exchange value: stocks and bonds, dollars, rubles, bitcoin, gold. In the middle of it all is a medallion, a coin of inestimable value representing nature that has not yet been plundered; the suggestion is that it will be soon. The commonweal is to be privatized.

Not all of Coe's art is so agitated or crammed with stuff. Some is straightforward, even spare, with the clarity of a declarative sentence. A boy stays the hand of a little girl reaching down to touch something lying amid flowers; the title reads "Don't Touch!" and the legend below: "Children against cluster bombs" (p. 145). Another print titled *He Incites Fascist Violence* (p. 98), shows Trump holding up a bible, as he did on June 1, 2020, in front of St. John's Episcopal Church near the White House, soon after cops violently cleared civil rights protesters from nearby Lafayette Park. The protesters are shown on their knees, with arms raised and fists clenched. Despite the tear gas, they have pulled aside their anti-Covid masks the better to be heard.

"It Can Happen Here"

"Birth of Fascism"

"Unpresidented"

"Court Capture"

"Eclipse"

"Swamp Street"

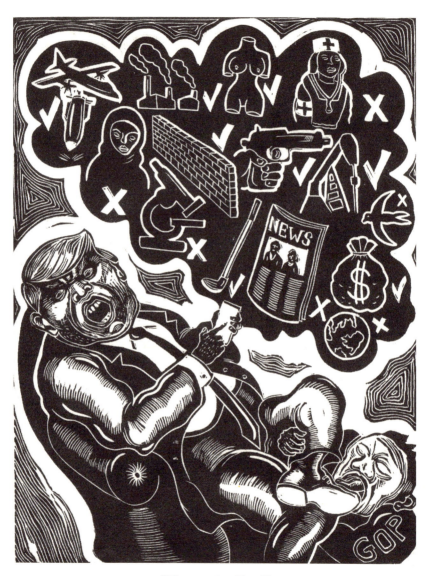

"Tweeter In Chief"

"Enemy of the People"

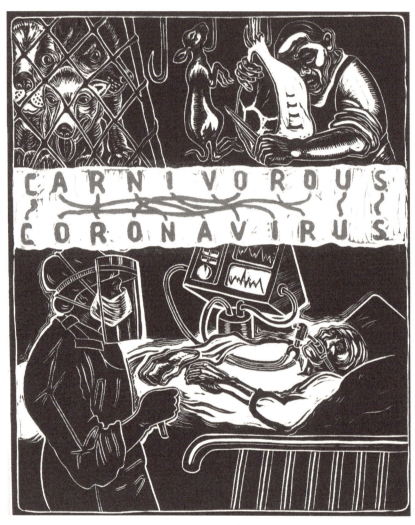

"Carnivorous-Coronavirus"

"Doctor MAGA"

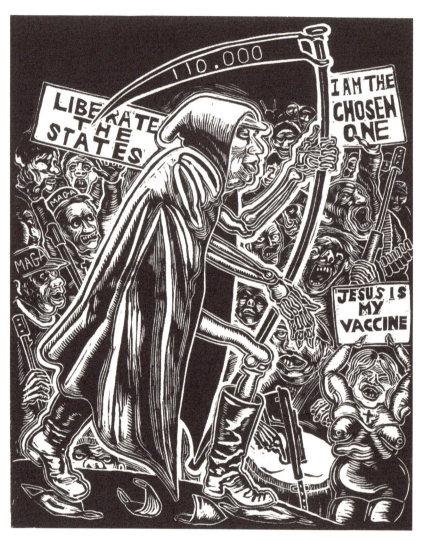

"The Dim Reaper"

"We Live in An Asylum"

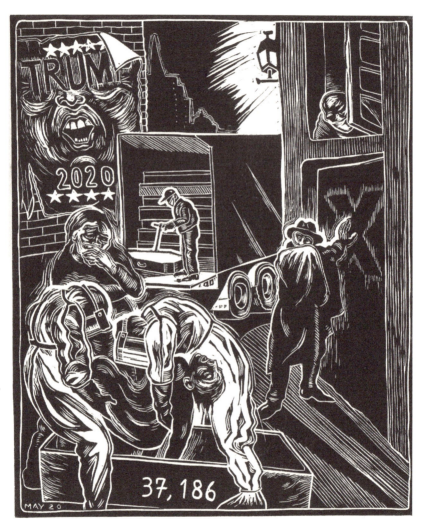

"Cardboard Coffins"

"One Million Dead"

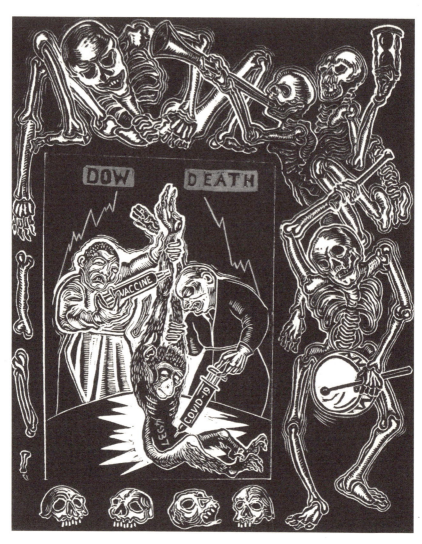

"Vaxx"

"First Known Case of Demon to Demon Transmission"

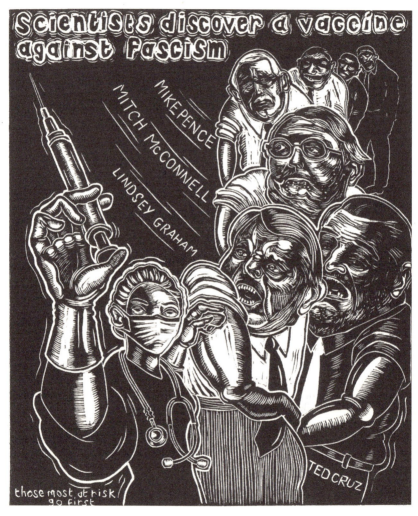

"Vaccine"

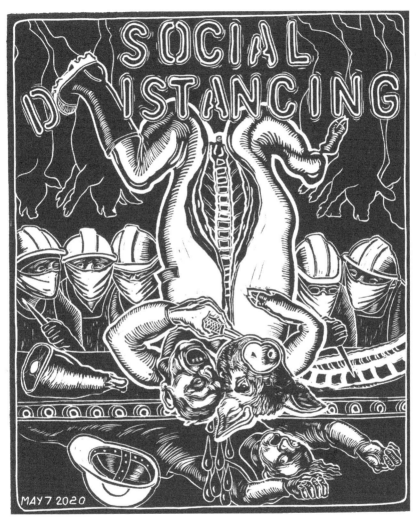

"Social Distancing"

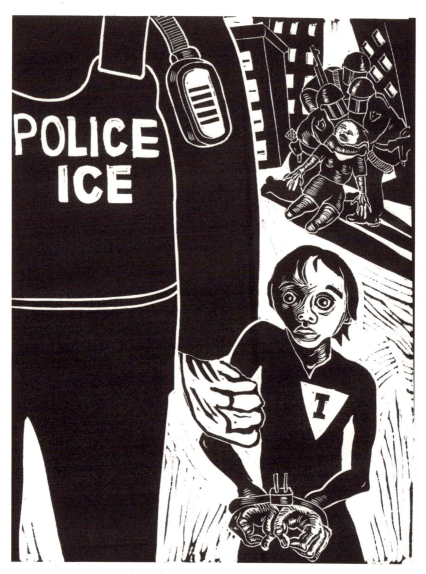

"ICE Baby"

"Rio Grande"

"Red Triangle"

"Bringing Into Conformity"

"Kongress"

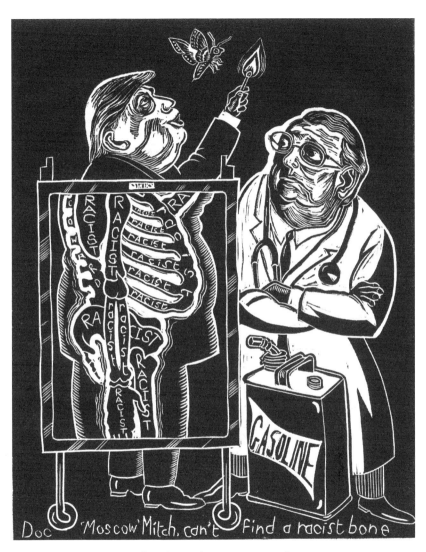

"Can't Find a Racist Bone"

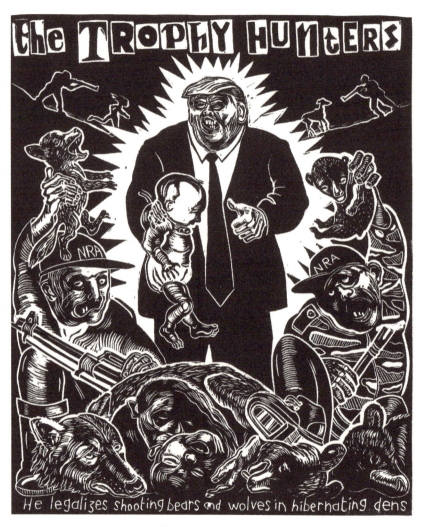

"Trophy Hunters"

"Gun Culture 1867–2023"

"Active Shooter Drill"

"Protect Children Not Guns"

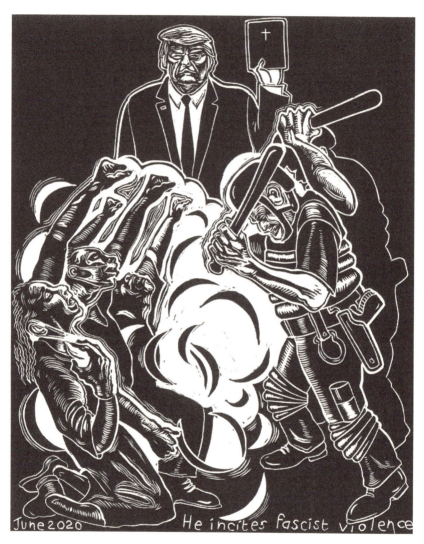

"He Incites Fascist Violence"

"Vermin"

"Impotus"

"The Other Shoe"

"Stop the Steal"

"Failed IQ"

"DeSantrump"

"Florida Laboratory of Fascist Politics"

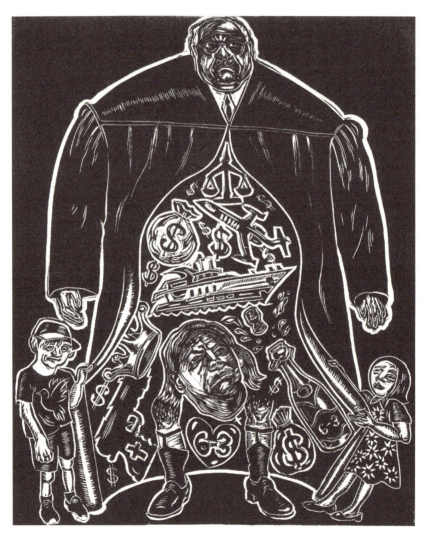

"Pull Back the Robes"

"Democracy Goes Under"

"Touchless Fascism"

THE STYLE OF POLITICS

Coe draws and sculpts her printing blocks easily and quickly. She has a mobile style—sometimes recalling the tenebrousness of Rembrandt's etchings and drawings, and other times the daylight clarity of William Hogarth's engraving; both are artists she adores. Like John Heartfield, another favorite, she marshals the short-cuts of montage, for example in *Enemy of the People* (p. 77), which shows Trump, Rupert Murdoch, and a shouting Fox broadcaster (his head inside an old TV set) overwhelming a climate protester holding a newspaper called *Daily Truth* with an illustration of a bee. (Bee populations are radically declining in the U.S. and around the world, due primarily to pesticides and habitat loss.)

In Coe's big drawing titled *War* (p. 139), she achieves the sense of scale usually associated with Hollywood movies of the golden era. She crams in as many people (including body bags), guns, tanks, aircraft, and buildings as she possibly can, from foreground to the horizon. There's no room to hide, retreat, or catch a breath. In the middle of the drawing is a woman on a stretcher attended by anxious friends or family. The motif recalls one found in Käthe Kollwitz's woodcut titled *Memorial Sheet of*

Karl Liebknecht (1919–20). Kollwitz's influence is also apparent in a drawing titled *Starving to Death* (p. 146), which suggests the death of thousands of innocent Palestinian children by focusing on a single, sitting girl embracing four emaciated animals. There is also a reference here to the image of an abused, fallen horse in plate two of William Hogarth's series of engravings called *The Four Stages of Cruelty* (1751).

"Easily Led"

"Woke Mob"

"Murdoch-Streicher"

"The Censor"

"The Censor" (printed on *Communist Manifesto* pages)

"Web 1" (words taken from San Francisco wall)

"Web 2" (words taken from San Francisco wall)

"Web 3" (words taken from San Francisco wall)

"Web 4" (words taken from San Francisco wall)

"Web 5" (words taken from San Francisco wall)

"Web 6" (words taken from San Francisco wall)

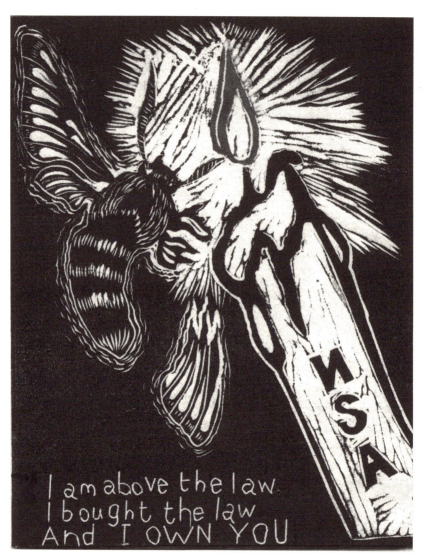

"Web 7" (words taken from San Francisco wall)

"Screen Shot"

THE CHALLENGES OF POLITICAL ART

Effective political art is hard to make. It requires, as we have seen, historical insight as well as finely honed craft. And even with these, there are significant pitfalls. Here are four common ones.

THE FIRST is bathos, the inadequacy of an artwork in the face of momentous events. The wars in Ukraine and Gaza for example, are so terrible, that in trying to represent them, the artist can seem overearnest or simply ridiculous. The solution is to filter such subjects through a mesh of metaphor and art historical reference. The result is mediated artworks that impacts viewers at the level of fundamental ideas. Sue calls these metaphorical compositions her "graphic" as opposed to "reportage" works, though both generally address significant political issues or injustices.

Sometimes, Coe combines the two modes. A recent example is *First Use of Nitrogen Gas* (p. 149), which depicts the killing of Kenneth Smith by the state of Alabama on January 25, 2024. Smith had been on Death Row since his conviction in 1988 for a murder for hire. (The man who paid Smith, the victim's husband, committed suicide before being arrested.) Though Smith was by all accounts a model prisoner, the state was determined to execute him: so determined, in fact, that they did it twice. The first time was by lethal injection, but they botched the job, and after about an hour, Smith was carried away semiconscious and returned to his cell.

The subsequent execution, by the novel means of nitrogen hypoxia, was more successful insofar as the patient on the gurney died, but not quickly or easily. He thrashed, choked, and vomited for at least ten minutes following administration of the gas. It was appalling. In her drawing, Coe departs from reportage in a few, key respects. First, she was not there, and for her, reportage means: "Being there. Drawing what I witness. Asking people to share their ideas and thoughts." In addition, Coe purposely took some liberties to make the image more complete: "I shook the scene around. It's not accurate. The nitrogen was in a different room but I wanted to show the tank. The mask is accurate. Full face. Priest 3 feet away." In addition, to avoid bathos, Coe made the scene a little bit mythic. Smith's arms are outstretched, as if he were being crucified or made a martyr. Here art historical references are evident, from *The Raising of the Cross* by Giulio Procaccini (c. 1620, National Gallery of Scotland) to the etching by Max Beckman titled *Hell (The Martyrdom)*, showing the murder by German government agents of the socialist revolutionary Rosa Luxemburg in 1919. The latter print is a frequent touchstone for Coe; like her drawings, it is intense, expressionistic, nightmarish, and purposely awkward.

THE SECOND risk faced by the political artist is melodrama, the exaggerated emotional affect that results from focusing on grief, pain, and suffering. A similar risk is sentimentality, the overemphasis of feelings at the expense of understanding. These can be overcome either by avoiding the most emotionally charged subjects—like dead or dying children and animals—or else by treating them (as suggested above) with the distance provided by art history and the subtleties of form. An injured or dying child, as in Coe's *Starving to Death*, is a melodramatic or sentimental subject. But because it is treated in a manner suggestive of Kollwitz, and deploys a complex and engaging formal composition, it may be seen as art, not just as the report of an atrocity. Coe may also use humor or irony—even in her darkest subjects—allowing viewers to gain emotional relief from a disturbing subject.

THE THIRD pitfall of political art is preaching to the choir, that is, attempting to persuade people to accept what they already believe. This is endemic in art today because of tribalism and identity politics. Progressives—Democrats, liberals, socialists, and others on the left—rarely stray from their own social, cultural, and intellectual circles; artists do the same thing. (This segregation, of course, is equally apparent on the political right.) The only way to overcome preaching to the choir is to undertake ambitious efforts to exhibit and publish in places where there is at least the possibility of reaching an ideologically diverse audience. This Coe does by producing designs for billboards, book jackets, magazine covers, and newspaper illustrations. She also frequently conducts print workshops at colleges and universities and donates works to human and animal rescue or relief efforts.

Another way of avoiding preaching to the choir is for the artist to become an investigative reporter, exposing truths that would otherwise remain hidden. Those discoveries then enter the store of general knowledge. About her *Gassing Hogs* (2010), for example, Coe has written: "I have drawn inside these slaughterhouses. Gassing hogs is less labor intensive (cheaper) than the single stun method, and is becoming, along with decompression for poultry, standard practice. Six hogs at one time can be stunned instead of one." Coe has been engaged with reportage almost since she was a child, growing up near a slaughterhouse in Tamworth, Staffordshire, England, and making art from her environment.

THE FOURTH and last hazard faced by artists who do political work is expiration. Any art that considers contemporary social or political issues runs the risk of becoming obsolete or outdated almost as soon as it's visible to the public; the issues might have been quickly resolved, or more likely, new crises commanded public attention while the old ones fade from view. The solution is for the artist to ensure that the political subject of her artwork is not merely a passing concern, but something structural that impacts a mass of people and will continue to do so unless settled. Coe also makes time-limited caricature, agitprop, or political cartoons. The point of these, and examples include *Enemy of the People* (mentioned earlier) and *Tweeter in Chief* (p. 76), is not to create museum-quality art so much as to summarize and satirize a particular instance of political idiocy, and then encourage a progressive audience to remain engaged with the question. And if an artwork sometimes expires, so be it, Coe can always make more.

"Mad Hatters"

"Q"

"Vote"

"Distrust"

"The Chorus Line"

"Stock Market"

"Abort the Court"

"War Stork"

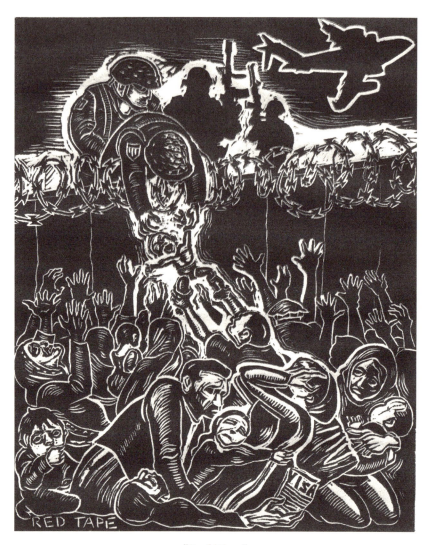

"Red Tape"

"Political Butchers"

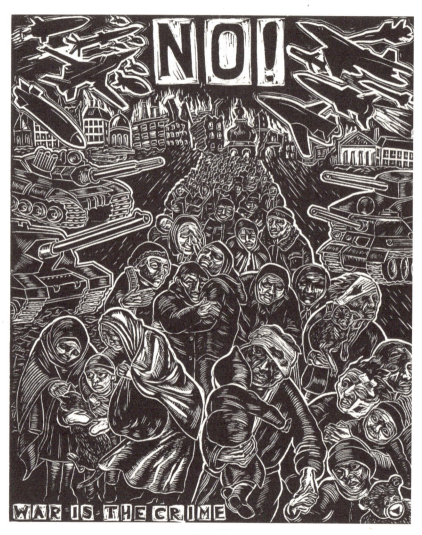

"No!"

"War"

"Civilian Deaths"

"Arms Merchants"

"An Explosion of Profits"

"Stop It!"

"Value"

"Don't Touch!"

"Starving to Death"

"UN Security Council"

"Stamped Out"

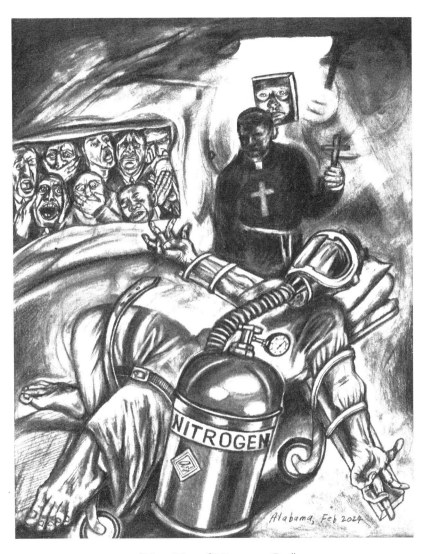

"First Use of Nitrogen Gas"

"Abortion Vigilantes"

"Forced Birth"

Economic Nationalism, a Dish of Alternative Facts

"Dish of Alternative Facts"

"Disinfo"

POLITICAL VS. "EXPRESSIVE" ART—AND THE END OF ART

Political art should be distinguished from expressive art; the former stages or makes possible an intervention into the domain of power, while the latter merely announces a position. The latter is far more common than the former. But the opportunity for artists to make a political intervention is greater than it may seem. Karl Marx once wrote: "The weapon of criticism cannot, of course, replace criticism by weapons, material force must be overthrown by material force; but theory also becomes a material force as soon as it has gripped the masses." Substitute the words "political art" for "criticism" and "theory" and the meaning of the passage in this context becomes clear: If a political artist produces something sufficiently incisive and engaging, it may serve to galvanize the masses and stir them to action. It's not only hunger, anger, and fear that sustain social movements; it is also understanding, imagination, and desire. That's especially true during times of upheaval or revolution, when a social mass is already primed for action.

Coe sets great store by this idea. She is one of the few major artists who is consistently engaged with social or political movements: human and animal rights, environmental justice, gender equality. Her art is also genuinely popular. To make sure it is seen, Coe publishes prints in relatively large editions and sells them for prices that ordinary people can afford. (You can buy an original print by her for as little as $60.) She also sometimes makes posters, billboards and even the occasional T-shirt from her original art. These translations from one medium to another aren't works of kitsch that condescend to their audience; they are efforts at creating popular art that meets its audience halfway, and raises its level of understanding and empathy.

For Sue Coe, the threat of fascism in the U.S. is more than just abstract. Her art focuses on those who are exploited and abused; decries state-sanctioned violence, whether perpetrated by the U.S. military or private individuals enabled by far-right politicians; celebrates physical nature and attacks the corporations that are destroying it; embraces the varieties of human culture, gender, and sexuality; and proposes that land and resources be shared by humans and animals alike. The name for such a system of mutuality, abundance and sustainability is democracy, and its prospects—along with the art that supports it—will be dimmed or destroyed if fascism is allowed to prevail.

"Animals' Warning"

"Wet Market"

"They Are Only Animals"

"Who is Selected"

"Ecocide"

"Air Quality"

"Child Workers"

"Greenwashing COP28"

"White House Erodes EPA"

"Insect Apocalypse"

"Cow in the Machine"

"Milk Thugs"

"Vanity Variant"

"Zoonosis"

"Sleepwalking to Extinction"

"If Animals Believed in God"

"Avian Influenza"

"The Mine in The Canary"

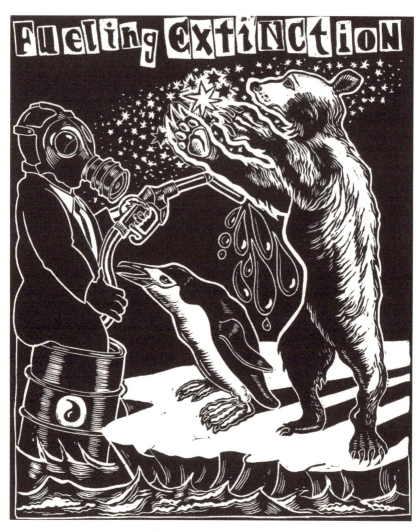

"Fueling Extinction"

"Climate Butcher"

"Empathy"

"Warning"

"If Bees Disappeared"

"Politicians Argue, Nature Acts"

"Justice"

"Guilty!"

"Hope"

"Men Have Died…"

"Children Are Weary of War"

"The Monstrous Choices"

"Proxy Wars"

"Reichstag Ear"

"RIP Hate"

SUE COE is an artist, animal rights activist, and anti-fascist. She is the author of *The Animals' Vegan Manifesto* and *Cruel: Bearing Witness to Animal Exploitation*. She has depicted the rights struggles of women, children, queers, animals, refugees, and political dissidents. She has exposed the suffering of AIDS patients, displaced persons, and domesticated animals. Her art has also exposed the horrors of factory farms, zoos, prisons, and refugee camps. Coe's prints, drawings and paintings are found in many major art museums, and her illustrations have been published in *The New York Times*, *The Nation*, and elsewhere.

STEPHEN F. EISENMAN is Professor Emeritus of Art History at Northwestern University and the author of a dozen books including *Nineteenth Century Art: A Critical History*, *Gauguin's Skirt*, *The Abu Ghraib Effect*, and *The Cry of Nature: Art and the Making of Animal Rights*. He is an art critic and columnist for *Counterpunch* and the co-founder of the environmental justice nonprofit Anthropocene Alliance.